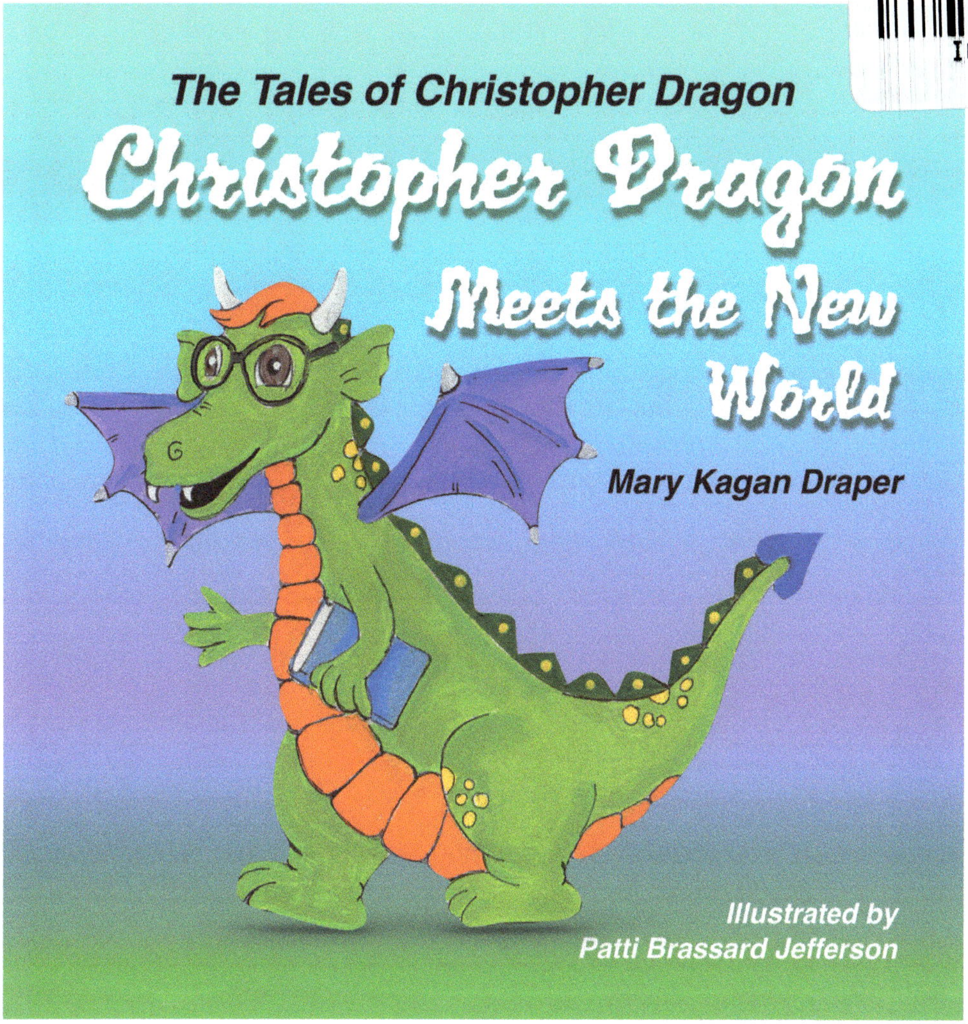

The Tales of Christopher Dragon

Christopher Dragon Meets the New World

Mary Kagan Draper

Illustrated by
Patti Brassard Jefferson

Copyright© 2014 Mary Kagan Draper
Illustrated by Patti Brassard Jefferson
All rights reserved.

No part of this book may be reproduced in any manner without the written consent of the publisher except for brief excerpts in critical reviews or articles.

ISBN 13: 978-1-61244-312-6
Library of Congress Control Number: 2014917231

Printed in the United States of America

Published by Halo Publishing International
1100 NW Loop 410
Suite 700 - 176
San Antonio, Texas 78213
Toll Free 1-877-705-9647
www.halopublishing.com
www.holapublishing.com
e-mail: contact@halopublishing.com

With love for my husband Bob, for his everlasting love, encouragement, and faith in me.

Here's a fun activity for you to do,
A gift from Christopher just for you.
On each page he has left a scale behind,
See how many of them you can find.

Christopher Dragon came to be
From a far off land across the sea.
He lived in the time of knights so bold,
Of kings and queens in the days of old.
He guarded castles and protected kings,
Keeping them safe from many things.

But soon those olden days were gone
And Christopher had to venture on.

Traveling through time and space,

Christopher sees the changes he will face.

Cars and trucks beep everywhere

While curious people stop to stare.

Airplanes, trains, and ships at sea

Are to Christopher a mystery.

Shopping malls, stores, and places to eat

Present Christopher with quite a treat.

A magic has sent Christopher into modern days,

Into a time of technological and computerized ways.

His life is much different than before,

When he lived amidst castles in the days of yore.

He found a cabin within the woods,

Where he lives among his store bought goods.

When a bath he must take,

He finds himself in a secluded lake.

His cabin is cozy, to say the least,

But rather small for a dragon beast.

Someday, a new house he may buy,

Deep in the woods where the trees grow high.

But now this new life is his to greet,
And every new day will present a treat.
The children will show Christopher what to do,
In this modern life, that to him is so new.

He exercises in a gym
To keep his dragon figure healthy and trim.
He works in a school library full of books,
Often having to explain his curious looks.

Christopher befriends children of all ages,

Together they read books while he turns the pages.

He explains the homework that they don't understand

And is always there with a helping hand.

Being a dragon of a magical size,

Matters not in the children's eyes.

Right from the very start,

Christopher Dragon finds a place in their hearts.

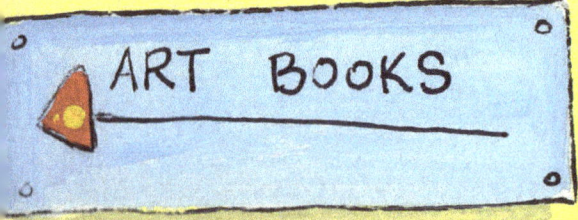

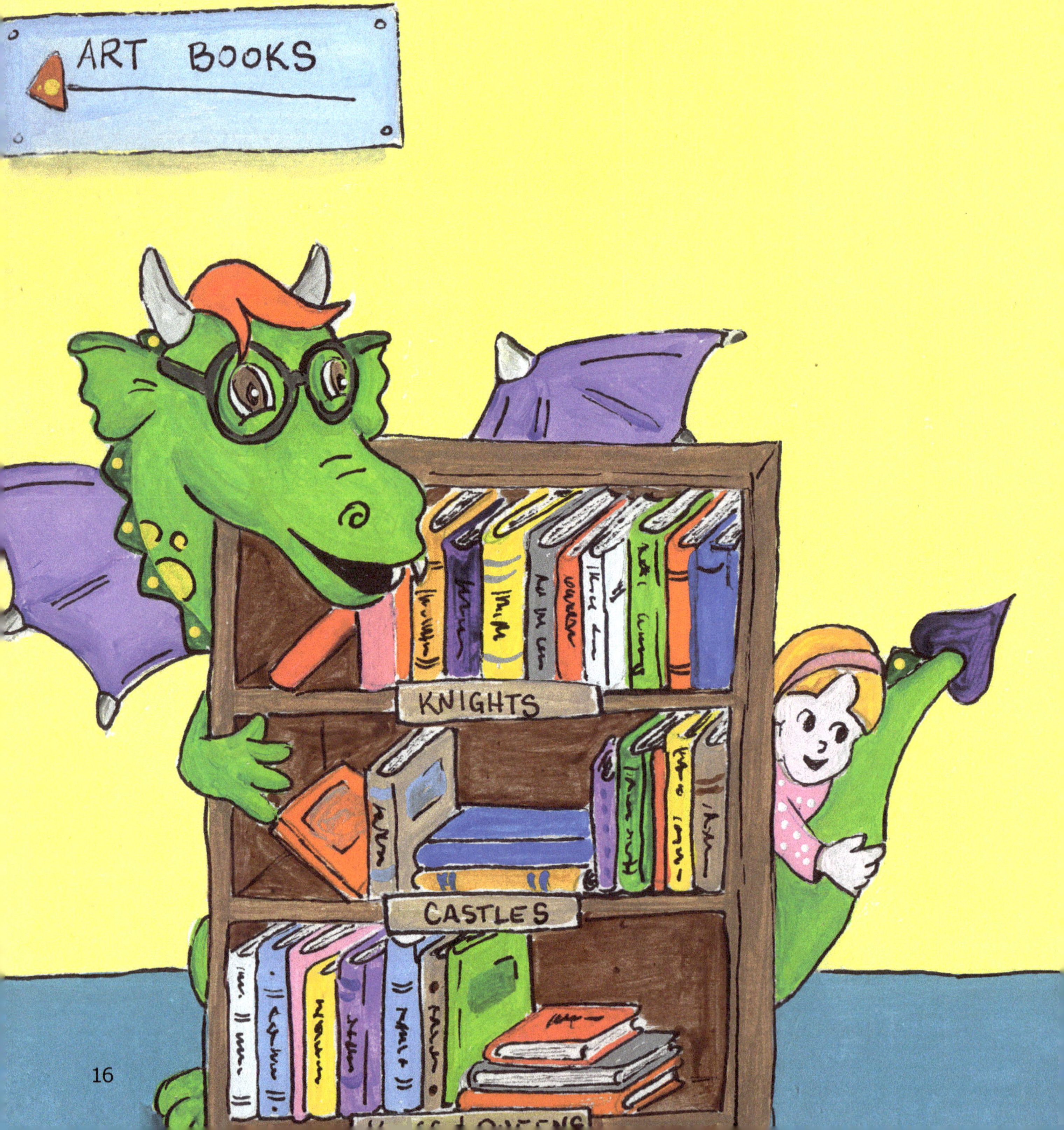
ART BOOKS
KNIGHTS
CASTLES

Children love their new dragon friend,
And the stories he can tell to never's end
They visit him in the library every day,
Often inviting Christopher to join in their play.

They sit upon his shiny scales,
And often hitch rides upon his tail!
He tells them stories and dragon lore
Of adventures he had where he lived before.

He types on a computer...

... and watches TV.

He goes to the movies for films to see.

He calls on his cell phone to make plans for the day,

And turns on the alarm when he'll be away.

He rides on a bus when the needs arise,

Often getting looks of curiosity and surprise.

Burger places are Christopher's favorite spot

To eat a fast food meal while it is hot.

Christopher can fly and spread his wings,

But his feet are made for earthly things.

Fire breathing he still can use

At any time that he might choose.

He has become a new dragon on the scene,

Quite handsome, in his coat of green.

A kindly soul who desires friends,

That he will take on adventures to this earth's ends!

www.ingramcontent.com/pod-product-compliance
Lightning Source LLC
Chambersburg PA
CBHW041439040426
42453CB00021B/2466

9 781612 443126